Plus

Health and Your Body

Science and Your Health

by Rebecca Weber

CAPSTONE PRESS
a capstone imprint

Pebble Plus is published by Capstone Press,
1710 Roe Crest Drive, North Mankato, Minnesota 56003.
www.capstonepub.com

Library of Congress Cataloging-in-Publication Data
Weber, Rebecca.
 Science and your health / by Rebecca Weber.
   p. cm.—(Pebble Plus. Health and your body)
 Includes bibliographical references and index.
 ISBN 978-1-4296-7130-9 (paperback)
 1. Health—Juvenile literature. 2. Medicine—Juvenile literature.
I. Title. II. Series.
 RA777.W435 2011
 613—dc22   2010034315

Summary: Simple text and color photographs illustrate the ways science is used to keep people healthy,
including medicine, X-rays, ultrasounds, and surgery.

Editorial Credits
Gillia Olson, editor; Veronica Correia, designer; Svetlana Zhurkin, media researcher; Laura Manthe, production specialist

Image Credits
Capstone Studio: Karon Dubke, Cover; Dreamstime: Darren Baker, 20, Mangostock, 7, Paul Landsman, 19,
Photoeuphoria, 9, Valerijs Vinogradovs, 11; Getty Images: Brownie Harris, 17; Photo Researchers: Peter Menzel, 15;
Shutterstock: forestpath, 1, Jim Barber, 21, StockLite, 13, wavebreakmedia, 5

Note to Parents and Teachers

The Health and Your Body series supports national standards related to health and physical
education. This book describes and illustrates how science keeps people healthy. The images
support early readers in understanding the text. The repetition of words and phrases helps early
readers learn new words. This book also introduces early readers to subject-specific vocabulary
words, which are defined in the Glossary section. Early readers may need assistance to read
some words and to use the Table of Contents, Glossary, Read More, Internet Sites, and Index
sections of the book.

Table of Contents

Science and Health

What does science have

to do with your health?

Doctors and nurses use science

every day to keep you healthy.

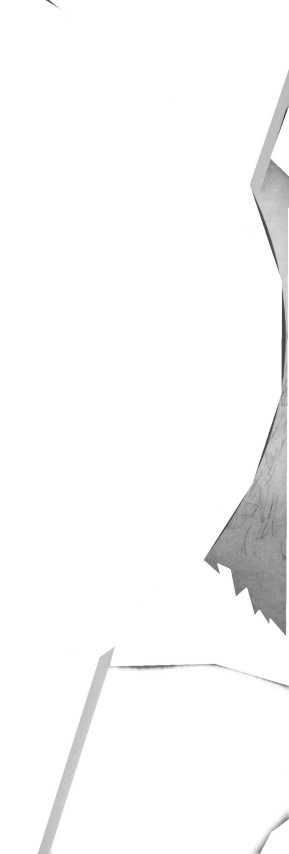

Helpful Medicine

Long ago, doctors used plants
to help people. Today, doctors
use all kinds of medicines,
but some still come from plants.
Aspirin is made from tree bark.

Some medicines are vaccinations.

Vaccinations teach the body

how to fight off certain diseases.

They keep people from getting

sick in the first place.

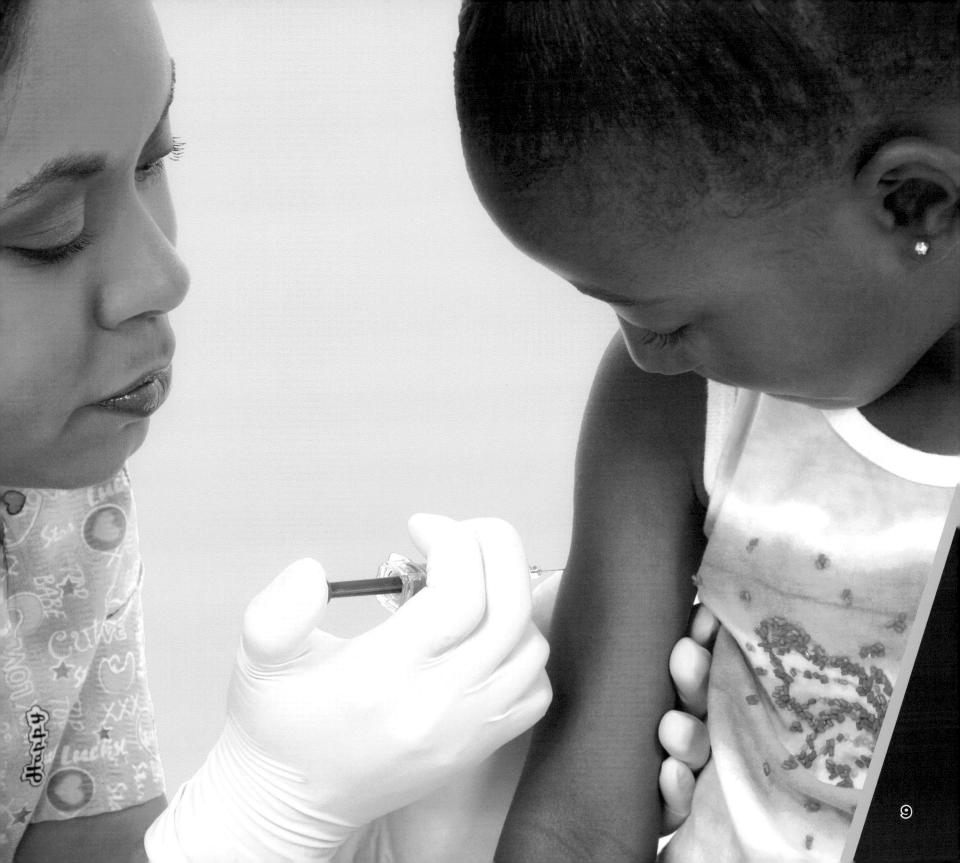

Looking Inside

Sometimes doctors look inside the body to help patients. X-rays are invisible beams of light. They pass through the body to create X-ray pictures.

An ultrasound also shows inside the body. This machine uses sound waves that bounce off things in the body. A computer turns the waves into a picture.

Surgery

Patients sometimes need

an operation, or surgery.

Some surgeries use robots.

A doctor controls the robot to

make tiny, exact movements.

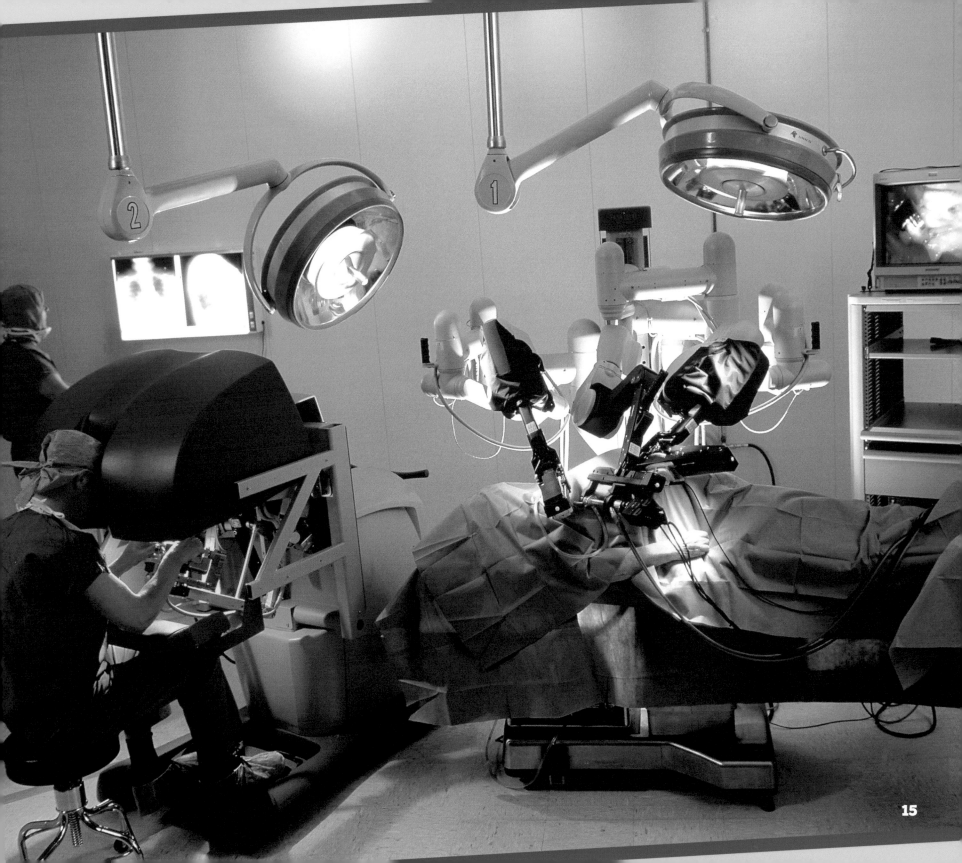

Most surgeries use knives,

but some use lasers. Lasers are

powerful beams of light.

They can fix weak eyes

or erase scars.

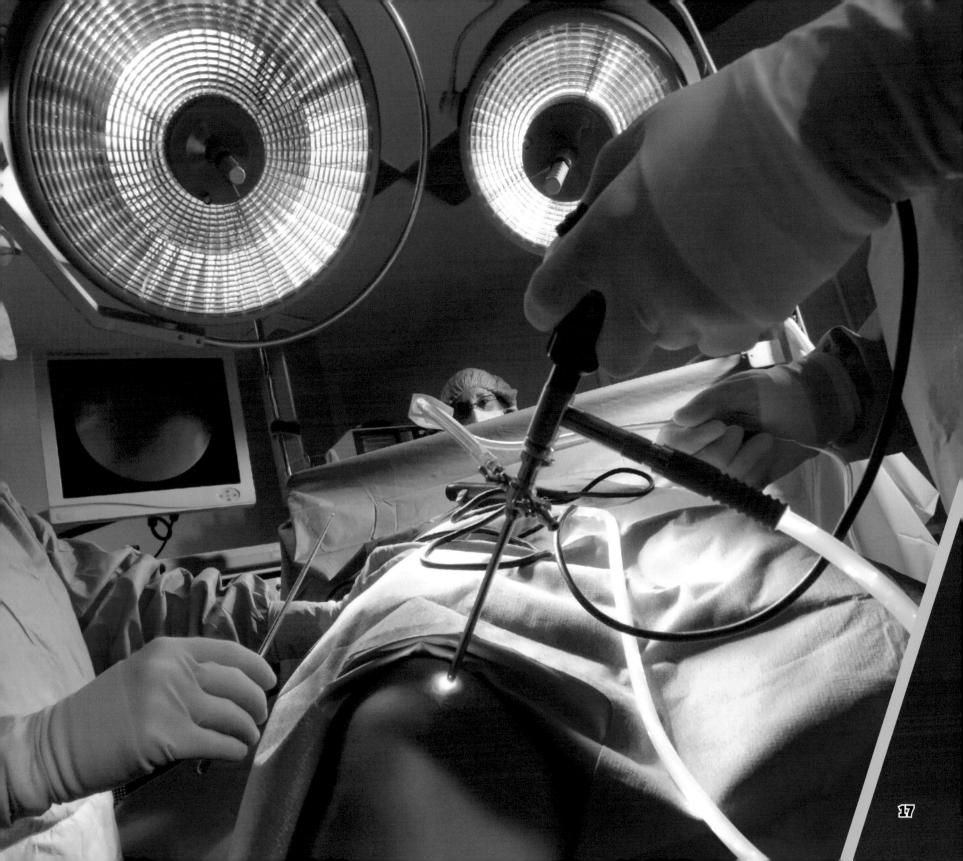

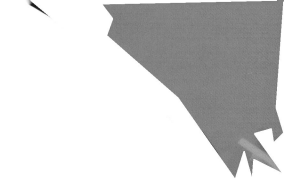

Doctors who do surgeries are called surgeons. They are always using science to help patients. They can even replace one person's heart with another.

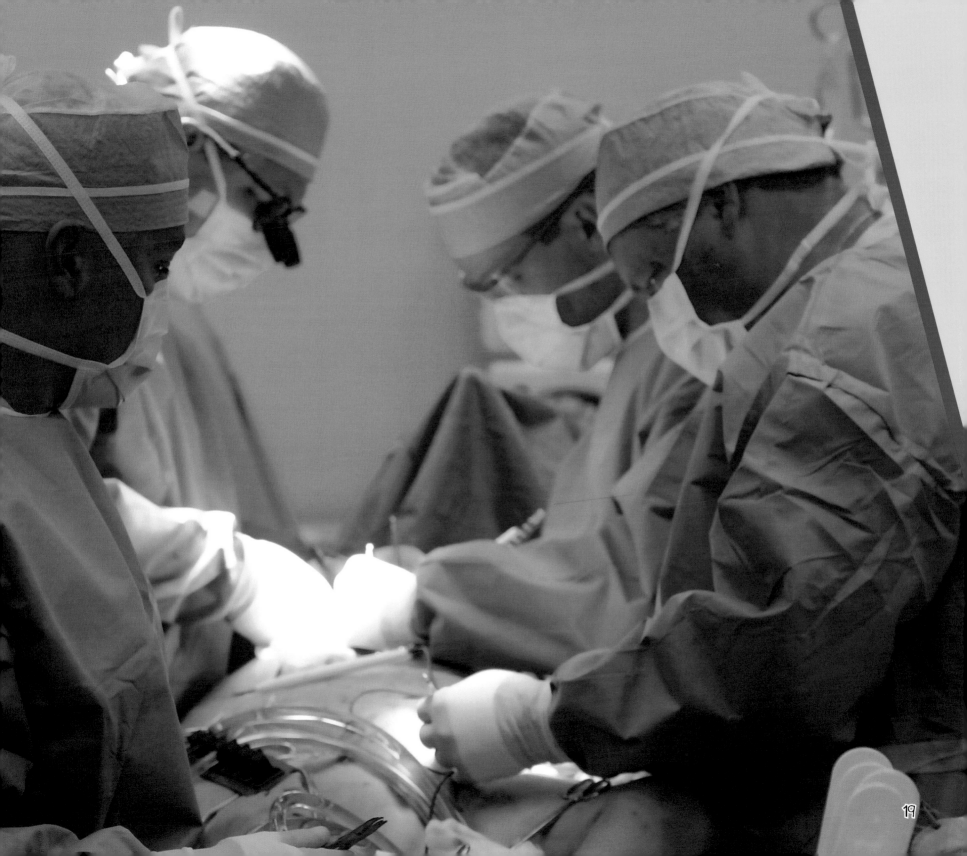

Fun Facts

- Microscopes were invented almost 400 years ago. Doctors use them to look at cells from inside a person's body.

- The first successful transplant of a heart from one person to another happened in 1967. It was done by a surgeon in South Africa.

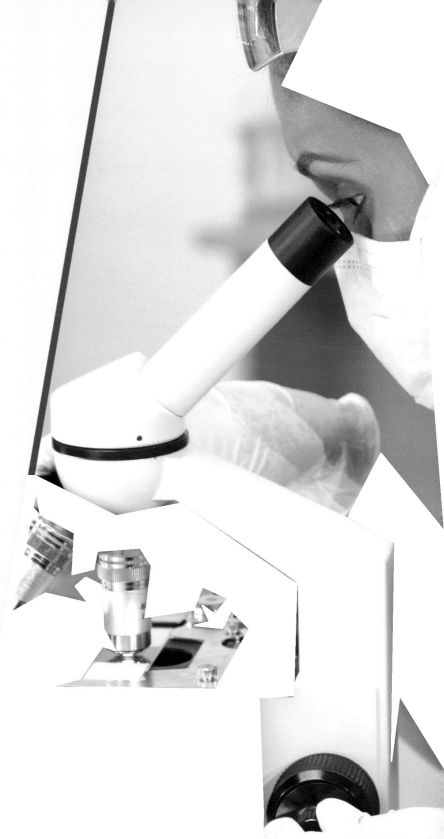

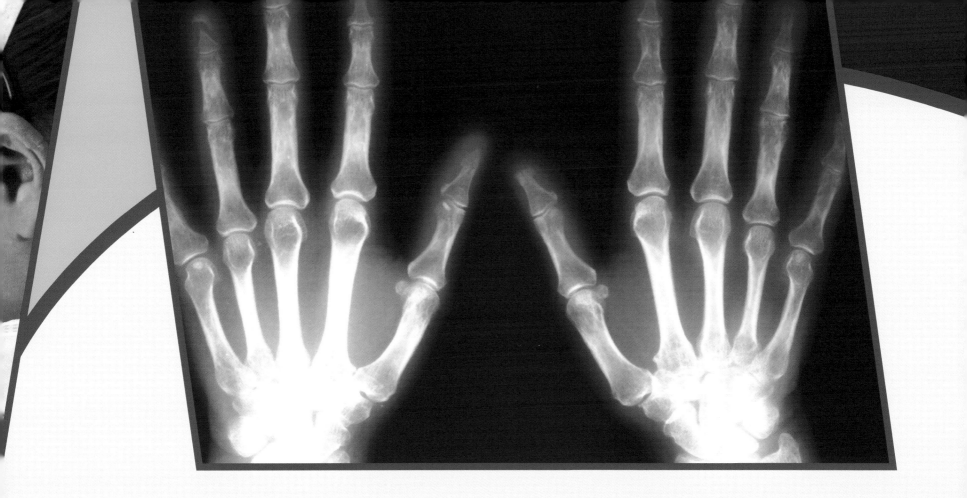

- At first, scientists did not know what X-rays were. They used "X" to describe the rays.

- X-rays can hurt an unborn baby, but ultrasound waves are safe. Many pregnant mothers first see their babies using ultrasounds.

Glossary

disease—a sickness

laser—a thin, powerful beam of light

patient—a person seen and treated by a doctor

robot—a machine that is programmed to do jobs that are usually done by people; a robot can also be directly controlled by a person

ultrasound—sound that is too high for the human ear to hear; ultrasound waves are used in medical scans

vaccination—medicine that protects from getting a disease, usually given in a shot

X-ray—an invisible high-energy beam of light that can pass through solid objects; X-rays are used to take pictures of teeth, bones, and organs inside the body

Read More

Fluet, Connie. *A Day in the Life of a Nurse.* Community Helpers at Work. Mankato, Minn.: Capstone Press, 2005.

Gorman, Jacqueline Laks. *Doctors.* People in My Community. New York: Gareth Stevens Pub., 2011.

Morgan, Sally. *How We Use Plants for Medicine and Health.* How We Use Plants. New York: Rosen Pub. Group's PowerKids Press, 2009.

Index

Word Count: 189 (main text)
Grade: 1
Early-Intervention Level: 21